Spells, Wishes, and the Talking Dead

ALSO BY WANDA JOHN-KEHEWIN

In the Dog House

Seven Sacred Truths

Published by Talonbooks

SPELLS, WISHES, AND THE TALKING DEAD

ᒪᒪᐦᒑᐃᐧᓯᐃᐧᐣ ᐸᑯᓭᔨᒧᐤ ᓂᑭᐦᒋ ᐋᓂᐢᑯᑖᐹᐣ

mamahtâwisiwin, pakosêyimow, nikihci-âniskotâpân

POEMS

WANDA JOHN-KEHEWIN

TALONBOOKS

Talonbooks
9259 Shaughnessy Street, Vancouver, British Columbia, Canada v6p 6r4
talonbooks.com

Talonbooks is located on xʷməθkʷəy̓əm, Sḵwx̱wú7mesh, and səlilwətaʔɫ Lands.

First printing: 2023

Typeset in Arno
Printed and bound in Canada on 100% post-consumer recycled paper

Interior and cover design by Typesmith
Cover image by Typesmith

Talonbooks acknowledges the financial support of the Canada Council for the Arts, the Government of Canada through the Canada Book Fund, and the Province of British Columbia through the British Columbia Arts Council and the Book Publishing Tax Credit.

Library and Archives Canada Cataloguing in Publication

Title: Spells, wishes, and the talking dead = Mamahtâwisiwin, pakosêyimow, nikihci-âniskotâpân : poems / Wanda John-Kehewin.
Other titles: Mamahtâwisiwin, pakosêyimow, nikihci-âniskotâpân
Names: John-Kehewin, Wanda, 1971- author.
Description: Title in Plains Cree syllabics unable to be transcribed. | Text in English with some text in Plains Cree syllabics.
Identifiers: Canadiana 20220496382 | ISBN 9781772015126 (softcover)
Subjects: LCGFT: Poetry.
Classification: LCC PS8619.O4455 S64 2023 | DDC C811/.6—dc23

Always for my children, my brothers, my beautiful mama, and Bird

"That's what's important really, Keeper says. Learning how to be what the Creator created you to be. Face your truth."

—Richard Wagamese, *Keeper'n Me* (1994)

LLᵘĊᐱ·ᕒᐱ·ᒍ mamahtâwasiwin Spells

ᐊᑯᕼᐱᒍˡ pakosêyimow Wishes

ᓂᑭᐢᒋ ᐊᓂᐢᑯᑖᐸᐣ nikichi-âniskotâpân The Talking Dead

FOREWORD

Throughout this collection I could feel the Ancestors and the sadness echoing through the generations. Beginning with a timeline, Wanda locates herself in the movement of time. These sparse historical details are an invitation to investigate further, while her poetry keeps us in the heart realm where the messages received cannot be discounted by the mind. There is nowhere to hide, the dead linger, and the loss of the children is felt:

> *unsaid goodbyes never again hellos,*
> *not able to hold their children again*

Wanda shares blood and bone memories in such a gentle way that they open us even further to the reality of the harm caused by colonization:

> *Being **nêhiyaw** is a career, always working towards survival.*

Survival that, for a time, brought the need to be other than what she was:

> *i stayed out of the sun*
> *wore green contacts*
> *learned vietnamese*
> *had half-vietnamese children*
> *stayed away from Powwows*
>
> *i was no wagon burner.*

We are reminded again and again of the differing world views and what was, for a time, lost:

> *Their grandchildren never hearing stories of how to be, how to walk softly.*

We find poems as prayers, calling to the dead. We feel the presence of her great-great-great-grandfather as his *hope travels through time* to lend his granddaughter strength. There is a humble, yet powerful, call to us to not look away. The call for action embedded in every piece:

> *But now, if you do nothing – I won't understand*

There is an acknowledgment of the cost of speaking out:

> *being a witness can be dangerous*

And a reclaiming of the teachings:

> *We didn't need to say sorry. We thanked*
> *we thanked   we thanked   we thanked*

We learn that Wanda will not be silenced:

> *what would you do if your only defence was*
> *a pen?*

She now knows that

> *all of this*
> *was not ours to bear*
> *and the shame of*
> *being born brown*
> *as over-ripened saskatoons*
> *was not a sin.*

Within this collection you will find a building of energy that culminates, becomes a crescendo calling to her great-great-great-grandfather and acknowledging that she is still a *newborn in healing,* that there is still *pain* but that she can see that *he is alive* in her daughter.

There is an urgency to these poems. Over and over she brings us back to the children:

> *no time to cry if you want*
> *to save the children –*

—**Jónína Kirton**

AUTHOR'S PREFACE

This book is divided into three sections: LL"ĊΔ·ŕΔ·ᴾ mamahtâwasiwin Spells, <d५⅄ˌ° pakosêyimow Wishes, and σΡ"ſ ⊲σⁿdĊ<ᴾ nikichi-aniskotapan the Talking Dead. The three sections are titled in ᴅ"Δ⅄∇·Δᴾ nêhiyawêwin and English. I examine the influence and meaning of language between English and ᴅ"Δ⅄∇·Δᴾ nêhiyawêwin. I use poetic elements, consciously using diction, meaning, English, and ᴅ"Δ⅄∇·Δᴾ nêhiyawêwin, trying to figure out what language means to poetry and what poetry means to language. I try to create a bridge between the two languages and create poetry that gives me some autonomy over my Indigenous heritage. ᴅ"Δ⅄∇·Δᴾ nêhiyawêwin does not use capital letters, which goes against English rules of grammar and syntax. Hence this book contains ᴅ"Δ⅄∇·Δᴾ nêhiyawêwin words that are not capitalized. I also intend to make sense of the guilt I feel as I write in English and struggle to name emotions, places, and things in ᴅ"Δ⅄∇·Δᴾ nêhiyawêwin.

This collection is about the grief I feel as I work to make sense of the world around me and my losses as an Indigenous woman. It was born from historical research, lived experience, and the personal need to reconcile the past with the present to understand what the future could be. As an Indigenous woman, I will always be on a healing journey with many questions, which I will always try to answer through various genres of writing. Writing acts as a therapeutic medium for making sense of intergenerational trauma resulting from colonialism. I attempt to show the correlation of reduced mental health within the colonial constructs of power and control over the diverse population and, in this case, the Indigenous population. The amount of grief, racism, and intergenerational trauma that Indigenous people have experienced and continue to experience is apparent in the statistics that show higher rates of alcohol and drug addiction, suicide, and incarceration. The urgency of these poems is to describe the hardships and the complex thoughts many Indigenous people have about how historical events still affect us today. My goal is to "stand in my truth" to pave the way for other survivors to stand in theirs. There is power in truth.

I do not claim to know exact dates and rely on dates found in the sources listed in the bibliography. I did rely on the internet for dates and found the research to be exhausting, as there are many different views, opinions, and details for every event, so please forgive me if I have misdated something. My only claim is that it all happened.

The timeline at the beginning of this collection provides the background for historical events and how those events have affected my life and my children's lives. I am a firm believer in trauma-informed practice and always look for ways to explain intergenerational trauma and outline how each historical event in Canadian history has affected Indigenous Peoples. I look at dates and set my Ancestors and parents within them; for example, my mother was born in 1952, and prohibition ended in 1961. My mother would have been able to go to pubs, whereas my grandmother, who was born in 1911, would not have had that experience. But did that mean my grandmother would have had a better chance of not becoming an alcoholic? Or did it mean drinking alcohol was forbidden and was done secretly and illegally?

Behind the Blue Quills residential school, where many children would try to run away in the winter

Photo by Wanda John-Kehewin

TIMELINE

The Fifteenth to Seventeenth Centuries

The **Doctrine of Discovery** is developed. It is used to objectify people and take their Lands if they are not Christian. It is also used to justify enslavement.

The concept of **Terra Nullius** is used by European powers to rationalize taking possession of Indigenous Lands. This continues into the twentieth century.

1665

Horses are first sent to New France, a vast area which includes three districts in Québec, as well as Hudson's Bay, Acadia and part of Newfoundland, and Louisiana to the south.

1763

The Royal Proclamation of 1763, issued by British King George III, acknowledges Indigenous Title and how this Title can be extinguished through the treaties.

Contrary to the Royal Proclamation, other European countries declare the land now known as Canada **legally empty** (see Doctrine of Discovery).

1831

The first continuously run **residential school** opens in Kanien'kehá:ka Territory. In 1922 the federal government takes over operation of the school. It closes its doors in 1970.

1871	Treaties 1 through 11 are signed from 1871 to 1921; the treaties were supposed to be in exchange for Land to be inhabited and used by "mainstream" Canadian society. Treaty rights typically provide for annuities, reserve lands, and trapping, gathering, hunting, and fishing rights.
Late Nineteenth Century	The federal government undertakes a formal partnership with churches to run **the residential school system.**
1892	The **federal government formalizes funding of the residential school system.**
1900	There are twenty-two **industrial schools** and thirty-nine **residential schools** in Canada.
1907	Dr. Peter Henderson Bryce, chief medical officer for Canada's Department of the Interior and Indian Affairs (1904–1921), reveals that **Indigenous children are dying at alarming rates** in residential schools in his *Report on the Indian Schools of Manitoba and the Northwest Territories.*
August 1911	**Mary Paul (Kokum) is born** near Onion Lake, Saskatchewan.
1918	**All Canadian women are given the right to vote except for Indigenous Women** – unless they give up their status, renouncing their Indigenous heritage in order to become enfranchised.

1920	Duncan Campbell Scott, deputy superintendent of the Department of Indian Affairs, makes **attendance at residential school mandatory for Indigenous children.** Scott wants to "get rid of the Indian problem" by enforcing attendance at residential schools until there is no "Indian in question," and no Indian Department."
1931	There are approximately **eighty residential schools in operation** in Canada.
1939	**Wanda's paternal grandfather Jimmy John fights in WW II** alongside approximately five thousand to eight thousand other Indigenous men. WW I and WW II allowed them to consume alcohol abroad, but not in the home country. Grandfather drank a lot, according to an uncle.
May 15, 1946	**Wanda's father Herman John is born** to Jimmy and Mrs. Jimmy John, a.k.a. Mary Paul.
February 25, 1952	**Wanda's mother Dorothy Boucher is born** to Henry Boucher and Cecelia Boucher, née Burnstick.
1960	Brings the start of the **Sixties Scoop,** which Wanda's mother is a part of. Many residential schools close, and Indigenous children are placed in non-Indigenous foster homes.
1961	**Prohibition is lifted for Indigenous people,** who can now drink alcohol legally. Dorothy and Herman are nine and fourteen; Mary is fifty.

February 11, 1968	Wanda's maternal grandmother dies (cirrhosis is listed as the cause of death). Dorothy is sixteen and is already in care.
1969	Dorothy is pregnant with her first child, a boy born in November.

Prime Minister Pierre Trudeau and Minister of Northern Affairs and Development Jean Chrétien announce the White Paper on Indian Policy, which uses the rhetoric of individual rights to rationalize assimilation. |
July 1970	Dorothy is pregnant with a girl; the intergenerational trauma flows from mother to daughter. Dorothy carries her mother Cecelia's trauma as well, which she also passes on to her daughter.
1971	Wanda John-Kehewin is born with all the eggs she will ever have; in the future she will pass on her epigenetic cargo of trauma to her children (intergenerational trauma).
1973	Wanda's last brother is born, and doctors force Dorothy to sign papers consenting to have her tubes tied.
1975–1976?	Wanda's maternal grandfather Henry Boucher dies by suicide (his daughter Dorothy believes). Before this, in July, he sends Dorothy and his grandchildren presents. Dorothy shares this revelation with Wanda when Wanda is twenty-seven.

1978–1979	**Wanda and two siblings go into separate foster homes,** both abusive placements down the road from each other, but they do not get to see their older brother. Sexual, spiritual, mental, emotional, and physical abuse is rampant in the homes.
1980	**Wanda is admitted to hospital** at nine years old for depression and suicidal ideation. By October 2022, Wanda believes this was a breakdown; only the doctor in charge of her care knows.
1980–1981?	**Herman and Dorothy divorce.** Herman chooses sobriety; Dorothy can't stop. Her past is too haunting.
1984	**Both Wanda's brothers attend Fort Qu'Appelle and Blue Quills residential schools.**
April 1985	**Bill C-31, the Bill to Amend the Indian Act, is passed.** This amendment addresses gender discrimination in the Act and restores status to women who had been forcibly enfranchised. Mom is eligible to apply for her status: her dad was enfranchised and her mom was Métis.
1986–1987?	**Wanda's paternal grandmother Mary dies** (of cancer?).
1990	**Blue Quills high school and residence closes.**
1991	**Wanda's first child is born.** Baby's first crib is an IGA cart. Wanda's first run-in with unconditional love.

1993	**Wanda's second child is born,** and she thinks she cannot give him the love and care he needs; as a survivor of sexual abuse … can she really take care of a boy? Can she be a good enough mother to him? she asks herself.
1996	**Wanda's third child is born** – how can she possibly care for such a perfect human being in an abusive relationship?
1997	**The last residential school closes.**
1997	**Dorothy tells Wanda that she should have no expectations and never be too happy,** because bad things will happen if she does or is. Dorothy says it's not as painful if you expect nothing.
1997	**Dorothy applies for her status and gets it.** She'd lost it earlier because her father was enfranchised.
January 18, 1998	**Herman dies of colon cancer.**
1999	**Wanda's fourth child is born.**
August 28, 2000	**Dorothy dies** all alone in the hospital from disease stemming from alcohol addiction.
2008	**The Truth and Reconciliation Commission of Canada is formed.**
June 11, 2008	Prime Minister Stephen Harper **apologizes to the former students of residential schools in Canada.**

2012	**Wanda's fifth child is born** into a calmer state of Wanda's life; however, she has anxiety about everything and is sensitive to sound.
2018	**Fifth child, who is six years old, comes home from school and asks if she will be sent to residential school** after learning about it at school. She cries and begs not to go to residential school. She cries herself to sleep.
2019	**COVID-19** hits. Fifth child stays home with Wanda for an entire year. She knows she is definitely not going to residential school. Daughter and Wanda spend quality time together, making their bond stronger.
2021	**Two hundred and fifteen unmarked graves are found** at the site of the former Kamloops Indian Residential School.
2022	**More than 1,100 unmarked graves are found** on the grounds of former residential schools, with more schools to search. Murray Sinclair declares that there were at least six thousand children who never made it home.
2022	**Wanda John-Kehewin graduates from UBC with her M.F.A.** and continues to write.

Gary Alteza, *Chief Big Bear 1887*, 2021

LL"Ċᐊᔨᐃ·ᑐ mamahtâwisiwin Spells

Mom was the fastest weaver at the weaving
factory where she worked

Photographer unknown

Dad

Photographer unknown

there's no ◁◁˙ᒉˑᒉᐢ awâsisak here

saskatoon berry juices run down silky-smooth sugar grin
rounded recognized treasured face dimpled in tang smiles and grace
tall grasses sway behind Child's silhouette
sun steadfastness devotion and ᓂᒪᒪ nimâmâ –

tiny muddy hands streak on Mama's expanse of width
that has held luminescent spirits in her Wombiverse
never knowing the future and not longing to know either
generous with love like it was the only truth and it was –

skinned knees and mosquito bites, lying in cool grasslands
looking up at Creator sky trusting it not to fall the only constant
trusting gravity trusting ᓂᒪᒪ nimâmâ to always catch you
when you fell and pick you up and that was yourstory –

chestnut hair in summer sun parted down middle of ᓂᒪᒪ nimâmâ's creation
two braids like freshly picked sweetgrass turning twisting complete
absorb steadfast sun who will always be there like nimâmâ
who knew how to braid hair because her ᓂᒪᒪ nimâmâ braided hers
and that was herstory and her mother braided hers and it was theirstory –

kisses upon satin saskatoon-soaked face
soft callused fingers slide and rest upon trusting back
shh   shhh   shhhh   shhhhh   shhhhhh   shhhhhh
like rain on empty teepee
like rain on empty longhouse
sh   sh   sh   sh
shhhhhhhhhhhhhhhhhhhhhhhhhhhhhhhhhhhhhhhhhhhhhhhhhh
tanned skin like sweet, ripened chokecherry
– nestlednexttomothernestlednexttofathernestlednexttograndmother –
nestled staring up at open skies into the night
admiring the sagging clouds that would always be there

deciphering ᖒᐦᐃᕀᐤ nêhiyaw shapes in sky
ᐚᐳᐣ wâpos
ᓯᓯᑉ sîsîp
ᐸᐢᑲᐤ ᒧᐢᑐᐣ paskwâw mostos
ᐊᐢᑭᐹᐘ askipwâwa
ᓂᒫᒫ nimâmâ
ᓂᐸᐹ nipâpâ
ᓄᐦᑯᒼ nohkom
ᒧᓱᒼ mosôm
untouched by (t)reason to create new ᖒᐃᕀᐁᐃᐧ nêhiyawêwin words
poof! poof! poof!
english
they cry for ᓂᒫᒫ nimâmâ in english.

they cry for ᓂᒫᒫ nimâmâ in english –

mud staining the faces of the unborn
leaving a trail of smeared mud body grooved drags –
even the Eagles cried and flew higher and stayed high
and the spiritually stripped followed suit and stayed high too –

there's no ᐊᐚᓯᓴᐠ awâsisak here

pressed flowers between waxed paper
melted into colonial preserves of cell-memory jam
hanging on by calcium-deficient fingernails and obligation
trodden lost spirits lifeless oppressed apparitions

disappear like smoke

poof!

there's no ᐊᐚᓯᓴᐠ awâsisak here –

Surrounded by White

i once tried to scrub my skin with brillo to wash my brownness away –
a little girl called me a wagon burner
we were only nine
what did wagon burner mean?
but the way it rolled off her tongue, i knew it was bad
the way the kids laughed
i knew it was bad
did they all know what that meant
like i'd burned a wagon? had i?
was coming from the reservation like burning a wagon?
i would find a friend in a plump white girl
who was also laughed at for being bigger

i knew being left out had something to do with the way my skin
turned a deep brown – red rose tea in summer
from playing out in the fields of jade blades and scorching sun
with all my other red rose tea cousins
playing cowboys and indians
not one wanted to play the part of the indian
because we knew they always got killed by the ᒨᓂᔮᐘᐠ moniyâwak
or thrown in jail and there was no real reason
the kids playing ᒨᓂᔮᐘᐠ moniyâwak would just chase the ᓀᐦᐃᔭᐘᐠ nêhiyawak
and we accepted it as such
ᐃᐢᑵᐘᐠ iskwêwak playing house and weaving tales
of hope and prayer to say we married white labourers

even the lighter-skinned ones would laugh at the darkest one
so aware of how lighter skin
was more beautiful everywhere
even on the rez

i stayed out of the sun
wore green contacts
learned vietnamese
had half-vietnamese children
stayed away from Powwows

i was no wagon burner.

∇ᒥᖴ ᐃ·ᔅᕐ∇·ᐃ·ᑎ

ᒧ"ᑐᣱ went to residential school
ᒐᕁᣱ went to war
ᐊ·"ᑯᒪᑲᑎ hung himself
ᓂᑲᐃ·ᐣ shot herself
ᓂᑲᐃ·+ drank herself gone
ᓂ"ᒪᐃᐧᐣ died with a bottle
ᒧ"ᑕᐃ·+ didn't want to die
ᓂᑎᑌᣱ lost to the streets
ᓂᑎᑌᣱ finally passed away
ᐊᐊ·ᕐᐣ lost to the system
ᓂᔅ witness and survivor

ᐊᕐᒐᐣᑕ∇·

mother's children final demise

how many tears did you weep
before you left us behind?

how many tears did you weep after?

trying to rid the political spiritual warfare monkeys
on your back   in your spirit
called you   no good
wrong colour   bad mother   heathen
savage   object   prostitute
drunk   addict   useless   indian

how many tears did you stifle?
held them like a dirty secret
blamed yourself

i am not normal   i am crazy   i can't keep it together
my children deserve better   their right   how can i love them if
i can't even love myself?   they're better off with the foster parents
i don't stand a chance   they know better than i do   i come from
some kind of fucked up   no one understands not even me my kids can't
even love me i'm so fucked up they deserve a better life than i could ever –
dirty secrets implanted there by bio-powers
used to take your kids from your spirit
from their spirit –

how many children cry for their mothers?
on naked pillows stained with ancient tears
in the homes of strangers who feel superior to your mother
children hold their tears inside like dirty secrets
i'm not good enough   she left because i'm bad   she doesn't
love me

she hates me   i'm bad   i'm bad   i'm bad if she loved me she'd
come back for me or fight for me   if she loved me   she'd fight for me
and they tell me it's all true
because you treat her like she doesn't matter
and she believes it
and if she believes it
her children believe it

how many mothers and children cry at night
looking at the same moon?

Monkeys in the Brain

I am fat
I am ugly
I am dumb
I am clingy
I am boring
I am worthless
I am a worthless Indian

I wear my trauma garlic
to the vampire party

no one will like me
why should they like me?

I am fat
I am ugly
I am dumb
I am clingy
I am boring
I am worthless
I am a worthless Indian

I wear my trauma cloak
to a baptism in hot sun

I am fat
I am ugly
I am dumb
I am clingy
I am boring
I am worthless
I am a worthless Indian

I wear my trauma smile
to Timmie's to order
triple triple
wait for them to discover
I don't have enough for coffee

I wear my trauma
deer in front of shotgun
trying to tame my fur
before I am shot

monkeys in my brain
at it again – you are good enough.
shh shhh shhh shhh
we're okay –

Smelling of Wine, Shame, and Sweet Sweetgrass

I remember the sporadic multicoloured flowers that grew out of hope and shit
In the fields of few and far between the precipices between
Yesterday now and never
Not knowing how long I was going to hang onto whatever
It was supposed to be that I was hanging
On for on the reservation where death of the invisibles is by your own "free will"
(huh?)

A child survives between wishful thinking, anxiety, and devastating reality made
of pure hope until one day she declares she isn't Indian and leaves it all behind.
She doesn't even pack a bag because she doesn't have a bag so leaves with her
hang-ten jeans on and knows anywhere is better than here.
She remembers how the aunties and the uncles came home walking up the
curved road, cigarette hanging from their lips like in an old western, returning
from a party – or jail. She remembers how loneliness settled on the reservation
like fog, everyone trying to outrun the pain with wine and sex because that's what
they learned when they came back from the schools that showed them how to
look in the mirror and hate that they were the wrong colour.

I remember them coming home smelling of shame, wine, and sweetgrass –

Confusion

Inspired by Layli Long Soldier's "Wahpanica"

I begin a line about the hill on my reservation tucked in between two towns that just tolerate waiting for a slip-up to attack **comma** to say *see I told you* **period** Nohkum and I used to pick Sweetgrass on the shaded side of St. Joseph's Hill on hot summer days next to a slough filled with ducks that came back from places I will never go **period** 1) I don't know where they fly in the fall **period** 2) I do not have dapper downy wings or natural instinct **period** 3) I am afraid to travel to places **period** I have gotten comfortable with the amount of racism here **period** Perhaps in other places there will be less tolerance for Indigeneity **comma** and I won't know how to handle that **period** Won't know how to fly away **period** 4) In hot places near the equator where they supposedly fly **comma** I may melt and never be put back together again **period** In hot summers here I am holed away in a dark basement with the fan running and white-noising my disassociation keeping me from melting into a puddle of unheard Ancestors' voices **period** 5) I am being held together by a frame of reference of what I can or cannot handle **period** Getting this far was already a journey around the stars of mental health and any sudden movements may shift the imaginary world I have so carefully put in place to catch me if I fall **period**

I wanted to write about kisêmanitow **comma** a word that when translated into English means the Creator of all things **period** Why is it every time I write Creator or God or kisêmanitow I feel the burning need to capitalize it **question mark** Is it because everything important to me has to be capitalized like Mom or Dad because they left me and left this world too soon or is it because of the rules of punctuation **question mark** Or is it because I do not want Creator or God or kisêmanitow to be angry with me **question mark** Is capitalizing a way for me to show their importance as if Creator or God or kisêmanitow would ever sit on top of St. Joseph's Hill **comma** cup of coffee in hand **comma** reading my poems to figure out if I always capitalized their earthly names **question mark** Perhaps Creator or God or kisêmanitow already knows what I am going to write before I even have the thought of writing it **comma** not sure if this punctuation should be a question mark or a period **comma** I don't have an answer either way **period**

I wanted to write about survivor's guilt **period** I wanted to write about a lot of things **period** The Ancestors **comma** my Parents **comma** my Nohkum **comma** my Uncles **comma** my Aunties **comma** my Cousins **comma** are no longer in this world **period** 1) Diabetes and colon cancer from eating flour **comma** sugar **comma** and lard **period** Eating treaty foods because it's all they could afford **period** Gone are the days of hunting for survival **comma** the supermarket filled with sweets and processed meats is the new way **period** Ever eat bologna fried in a pan alongside askipwaw **question mark** askipwaw translated means Earth's egg **comma** translated again it is just potato **period** Survival of the fattest **period** 2) Alcohol became the new Ceremony for hurting hearts because the real ceremonies became a pastime instead of a way of living **period** 3) Violence is a side effect when everything is taken away and you don't even have your kisêmanitow-given name and you are wearing someone else's shoes because you can't afford new ones or you feel like you don't deserve new things because no one else can afford them **period** 4) Suicide became an option after language **comma** Culture **comma** tradition **comma** ceremonies became something you only knew the words for in another mother tongue **comma** not even your own as the words rolled across your tongue and the roof of your berry-stained mouth still sounding so foreign **comma** a rez accent still vibrant **comma** leftover from our old language **comma** and instead of feeling shame for having a rez accent **comma** we should feel proud because we still have remnants of how our language used to sound **period** It's not because we're stupid **period**

kisêmanitow **comma** a word I learned recently and before that only knew God as we trudged to the old white church that could hold fifty converted catholics on a cold sunday morning for communion or a hot friday afternoon for a funeral of another Child or another Elder **period** We would all gather under the roof and steeple and say our hellos and goodbyes and niceties about the weather and what a good person so-and-so was and how much they will be missed in a community that's losing more than it is gaining **period** The death rate is higher than the birth rate **period**

Gone are the days I could sit in tall grasses thinking of my next story or next poem to share with my community sitting around a fire **comma** time not existing for the sake of controlling the world **comma** controlling destiny **period** Why do we laugh at the youth when they mispronounce a Cree word instead of embracing them and gently helping them pronounce beautiful words in Cree **question mark** Why must I always write in english splashed with a few Cree words like spices in a quickly made stew **question mark** Why must I feel guilty relaying thoughts in English and publishing like a traitor **question mark** Perhaps my poems translated from English to Cree don't make sense **period**

Are there even periods in the Cree language **question mark** Or am I stopping a life cycle of words **comma** a continuation of thought that flows forever and is passed on to our children through story and more story **question mark** or **period comma** freedom of choice **comma** you decide **period** There is no word for goodbye in Cree **period** Nothing is as final as goodbye **period** New words had to be created when two worlds collided like spirit and stone **comma** both sides trying to survive in the ways they knew to be right **comma** in the ways they were raised **period** The period stops me from rambling on **comma** rambling into territory comma stopping my ideas from flowing **comma** like I have to stop **period** The cycle of oral tradition stops with each period end stop forcing me into a new way of thinking **comma** like I could change my mind anytime instead and change the story **comma** change the direction of old stories not meant to be changed **period**

Would my words in English translated to Cree make any sense **question mark** Or would it sound like someone lost in the past of sadness **comma** betrayal **comma** and anything but mindfulness **question mark** How will I ever know that if I do not speak my language **question mark** A good Cree joke told in Cree translated to English is not funny anymore **comma** but instead becomes contention for the Cree speaker trying to relate it to you in English and you're left with a longing and a lack of belonging **period** I know I speak Cree somewhere in my body **comma** but my tongue doesn't remember how to roll the heavily accented words off my assimilated tongue **period** Is language the way back home **question mark** The way back to a sense of connecting to the ways of the land **comma** to the language of the land **question mark** Will I ever know **question mark** Will I die not knowing my language **question mark**

êtikwê wiyasiwêwina

nohkom went to residential school
mosôm went to war
wahkômâkan hung himself
nikâwês shot herself
nikâwiy drank herself gone
nôhcâwîs died with a bottle
nohtâwiy didn't want to die
nitôtêm lost to the streets
nitôtêm finally passed away
awâsis lost to the system
niya witness and survivor

âcimostawêw

My Purse and COVID

MY PURSE	COVID
An empty old bubble gum bubble pack wrapper	From a time I can't recall
An old elastic with strands of hair	tangled like weeds
An old restaurant receipt	before COVID
An expired licence with a mug shot	fading from wear
A wallet from village value with no money	falling apart at the seams
Old mascara past its two-year throwaway point	for no reason at all
An old cherry chapstick with grains of sand	no idea how this came to be
A used mask for just-in-case moments when	I need to breathe carefully
An old eyeliner smudging the translucent cap	Waiting to be tossed
An old travel brochure for an Alaskan cruise	Like I could ever afford it
A pack of cigarettes and a lighter	My sanity entwined in smoke
A pink highlighter from UBC	Not sure when normal will be back
Crumbs from some unknown dessert or beach	Not sure if I'll ever find out
An old eyelash curler with missing rubber pads	I should probably retire
An old toys "r" us card from Christmas shopping	I will not collect points
A dime from 2010 when I was thirty-nine years old	That I will never get to spend
An old ballpoint pen missing the ball	What or where's the point?
An old hard copy picture of my daughter at sixteen	Eyes full of trepidation
	of the future
An old picture of my son at nine with a seal	Cringing and holding shoulders tight
A boston pizza menu with gluten-free pizza	Waistline begs to differ
A bottle of expired advil	In case of an apocalypse
A letter from the cra saying I owe money	I will survive

Get Messy in This Moment with COVID on the Horizon

This moment in time, I sit here answering my daughter's questions over and over, as I trail behind her cleaning sprinkles of flour and grains of salt all over the floor left from her trying to make a dumpling in the microwave out of a mixture she made which resembles playdough – she asks me to try a bite and I do because at this point, seeing her disappointed face isn't on my list of things to do or fix today. It tastes like playdough and I imagine her petting the two dogs and the two cats before she gets down to business and kneads a little dough ball the size of a small delicious plum. Only this isn't a delicious plum. This is a creation made by a daughter who is bored out of her mind, who is staying home with Mom, two dogs, two cats, a gecko, and her older brother who stays in his room most of the time, even before COVID.

I am trying to keep up with my schoolwork as we fall behind in hers and still her smile as she makes herself a melted cheese sandwich in the microwave for the first time today – and just how proud she is as she hands me a small corner of it, and I bite it knowing her hands probably taste like salt from the playdough plum dumplings she tried to make a little earlier. I am in the same room as she does all this and I offer spare words of advice tossed over my shoulder and little watchful looks from my screen to her and her unicorn shirt, like only thirty seconds, not too much salt, wash your hands, try not to get the flour on the floor, and watch out it's hot, and I declare I'll do the honours and cut the crusts off.

Many times throughout her eight years on this suffering mother earth, I have stood by the microwave watching the plate spin as her cheese melted. For some odd reason, my beautiful child likes to eat melted cheese (we call it) and it's not a "real" melted cheese if it doesn't have two slices of fresh, soft, white bread. Melted cheese is my usual thing … but today she looks at me typing like my life depends on it, and I really think it does, I think she gets a moment of clarity and compassion for another person as she asks me, "Mommy, tell me how to make melted cheese, I can do it." And still a barrage of questions assaults me – Can I use two cheeses? Can I cut off the crusts if I use a butter knife? How 'bout a scissors? How long do I put it in for? Did you make melted cheese when you were small? I shake my head and I do not tell her; we didn't have a microwave and my mom left me when I was five. That's another story for another time that doesn't have any melted cheese in it, but it does talk of melted lives and hearts.

I let her make her playdough plum dumpling because who am I to stop her from keeping her mind busy as I see the wheels spinning in her perfect head as she sees her little dumpling spinning round and round in the microwave looking more like the crusts left over in a used bannock bowl left overnight.

She is eight and missing out on very important relationships, very important lessons in schools about the art of being with other human beings and learning to navigate the world around her. How can I, a survivor of trauma, teach this little one that the world is not a place to fear when COVID just kicked the world in the royal pain in the ass with a fuck-you boot?

How many parents, besides me, feel inadequate and are worried we will mess up our children? We all, as a universe without any soul connectivity, bumbled our way through 2020, 2021, and 2022 – hoping and probably no longer praying for COVID to be ~~manageable~~ DEAD and a thing of the past like children's childhoods of 2020, 2021, and 2022.

Hopefully all of our self-isolating will keep us safe, and handwashing isn't as important if we stay home and pretend the world doesn't exist. I say to myself and to no one in particular, except on this fresh page: I don't know if I can do it. But whatever else choice do we have as my daughter grows up isolating because she must and me isolating because I want to. We are like vampires in the night on our evening strolls to take our dogs to the park, avoiding people. ~~like the plague.~~

Only Half, and Maybe Not the Right Half

Leigah Keewatin, *Wolf & Moon*, 2022

Wolf head burned into maple
like old cigarette burns on the roof of my car
the one I promised I'd never smoke in.
Age lines and wooden wrinkles weave through wolf
created in Somerset, Manitoba, in 2018.
Salmon coloured lines, burned Braille
so perfect in the imperfect

and we forget that about ourselves
as we step on scales and lather eye cream
like lotion on new baby or new babe
so slippery, like descaled fish.
Someone's second love
someone's second passion as
dust swirls in triangular light
from cat-shaped wrecked blinds.
Burned cinnamon into specks that
give both the eye and the brain
closure. Art will save us.
Books of poetry on the "to read" shelf
two sharp pointy teeth, gnawing on folded corners
wood or book.
Two sharp pointy teeth against maple cookie
egg-shaped moon. Institutional tan walls
Like the office of a counsellor
who has not healed either
and labels you.
Not holes to get lost in
if you look close enough.
Tiny pinprick holes in walls
from to-do lists never read
someone's meditation
just not mine.
ARTist sees mistakes
must live with them
or give it up.
Whiskers on a loved father
or uncle
who have both passed on.
Wolf howls at moon

silhouetted by egg-moon maple-cookie colour
black knots like moth wings
animals get tired too.
Smells dead
forever.
Someone's entire essence in each stroke
Someone's entire life in each poem
a piece of their energy spread across the universe.
This artist knows someone who
died of cancer.
Knows someone who was too tired.
The perfectionist in me wants to fix the moon.
Fix the cancer. Fix colon-ization.
Perfect in the imperfect
and yet I need control of my environment.
Pyrography as trauma's braille
only the soul can read
closer to letting go
colonizing the wood.
Dried baby umbilical chord
struck and floating
child wandering the world
lost.
Signs of waterlogging
traumalogging
from a survivor
certificate of authenticity
remembering one matriarch
who made the difference.
Signed white paper like broken treaty
Indian spirit left on the plains
to wander – lost umbilical chord.

Shamefeeding

The ▓ first time I saw my ▓ child, ▓▓▓▓▓ I was afraid ▓▓▓▓▓▓
with shaky arms, tears ▓▓▓▓▓▓▓▓▓ thoughts ▓▓▓▓▓ raging
▓▓ questioning whether ▓▓ I·could ▓▓▓▓▓▓▓▓ not leave like my
mother did. ▓▓▓▓▓▓▓▓▓▓▓ healing ▓▓▓▓▓▓▓▓▓▓
▓▓▓▓▓▓▓▓▓▓▓▓▓▓▓▓▓▓▓▓▓▓▓▓▓▓▓▓▓▓
▓▓▓▓▓▓▓▓▓▓. How was I going to do that?
▓ the nurse brought her to me, ▓▓▓▓▓▓▓▓▓▓▓▓▓
▓▓▓▓▓▓▓, I was afraid to break her. Afraid to love her. ▓▓▓▓▓
Afraid to lose her. Afraid. ▓▓▓ the nurse tried to ▓▓▓▓▓▓▓▓▓
▓▓▓▓▓▓▓▓▓▓▓▓▓▓▓ touch my body without asking?
▓▓▓▓▓▓▓▓▓▓▓▓▓▓▓▓ to help me get my daughter to latch.
Latch. Latch. Latch. To what?
Latch?
I've never latched to anything –
So we tried. ▓▓▓▓▓▓▓▓▓▓▓▓▓▓▓▓▓▓▓▓▓▓▓
▓▓▓▓▓▓▓▓▓▓▓▓▓▓▓▓▓▓▓▓▓▓▓▓▓▓▓▓▓▓
▓▓▓▓▓▓ This nurse ▓ was trying to shove my breast into my baby's mouth
like she could force-fit us together like two Duplo and Lego ▓▓▓▓▓▓
▓▓▓▓▓▓▓ Incompatible like hardened clay, all grey and depleted and new
clay trying to find a sense of belonging first ▓ force-fed by a nurse ▓▓▓▓▓
▓▓▓▓▓▓▓▓▓▓▓▓ as she cooed at you like she was trying to engrain
her colonial voice into your brain for future oppression and brainwashing.
▓▓▓▓▓▓▓▓▓▓▓▓▓▓▓▓▓▓▓▓▓▓▓
▓ the pervasive feelings rising in my body, ▓▓▓▓▓ smoke from a burning bog,
reaching my stomach, my throat, my thoughts ▓▓▓▓▓▓ stop. ▓▓▓▓▓▓▓
▓▓▓▓▓▓▓▓▓▓▓▓▓▓▓▓▓▓▓▓▓▓▓
This was not normal.
The shame ▓▓▓▓▓▓ my body … running, coursing … running coursing
through my body. I did not want to taint ▓▓▓▓▓▓ with my body that had been
ravaged, pillaged, ▓▓▓▓▓▓▓▓▓▓ I ▓▓▓▓▓▓▓ will not ▓▓▓▓ place
my tainted broken body near her. She was too pure. The shame spread across
many generations ▓▓▓▓▓▓▓▓▓▓▓▓▓▓

██

████████████████████████████████ I could not feed her the shame embedded
in my DNA.
██

██

██

███

████████████████████████████████████

██████████████████████████████████████

██████████████████ they used to help their

If a Child Falls in the System Does Anybody Hear?

I fall

I crawl

I feel

finally

I breathe

as my children

walk out the door –

Old enough not to be snatched –

Trauma that courses

through my veins

courses through their veins.

Trauma bond hardened

by broken clocks

missing hands

missing decades

missing family

screaming silently.

A time loop of black magic

as if there's room for judgment

at someone who screams

when their world falls apart

as you lead their children out of the house.

And in the beginning, the word was

supposedly god

apparently but in what language?

Must have been ᐲᐦᐃᔭᐍᐏᐣ nêhiyawêwin

as my children walk out the door

Too old to be snatched –

I breathe –

And in the beginning the word was ᑭᓭᒪᓂᑐ kisêmanitow.

Probably Politics

Grandmother went to residential school
Grandfather went to war
Cousin hung himself
Aunt shot herself
Mom drank herself gone
Uncle died with a bottle
Dad didn't want to die
Friend lost to the streets
Friend finally passed away
Child lost to the system
Me witness and survivor

She tells a story –

we tried

we eat in darkness
part the silence
with small talk
about the coworkers'
argument.
we never get that bad
as you grapple your steak
with a butter knife.
braindeep in poetry
i wished you would shut
the sound of the news
sirens and air horns
Some people don't want to cry
Some people still want to believe we'll survive

Us or the world?

Certainly not both.

Give Us Our Daily Bannock

I carry upon my shoulders
the need to redeem my mother for leaving
she was a red-gold god unrealized,
trauma bond intact like a gift for me
because I'd always hang on –

The dis-ease of trauma
planted deep in brittle bones
that took over broken bodies, like smallpox –
scattered, scorching, sad souls searching.

Systems of oppression occupying
space and position
genocide a necessity written by man
when jesus roamed the Earth:
Apparently that led to the slaughter
of millions across Turtle Island
and in return
treaties   and   flour   and
sugar   and   oil   to   make   fried   bannock

A survival of the fattest greasy mark of oppression
on the lips and chins of future children.

Heartbeat of the Drum Calls Us Home –
Not Everyone Hears It

About twenty-two years ago, I see her hurriedly walking down Hastings near Main Street on an overcast fall day, wind whipping leaves into imaginary cones of silent chaos. I don't remember where I was going but I imagine it might have been to Battered Women's Support Services, a support group for women in abusive relationships. We were both trauma survivors, intergenerational trauma receivers, and Indigenous.

I recognize something familiar about this woman walking and that familiarity of safety floods through me like a beacon of refuge as I drive past lost people struggling to survive. My heart must have been heavy, as it was the year my dad passed away. Seeing my friend brings me some hope, I see her and perhaps she can be there again for me is what I know I feel. She has helped me so much in the past, so I am hoping she can help me again, or so I think in a split second. I see my friend I haven't seen for at least five years who one day just disappears and the last time we talk, she tells me she's sorry, sorry she left. This day embedded in memory as I stop my car and call out to her, "J!," the too-thin shell of my old friend stops, looks in my direction, and heads towards me, her extreme weight loss painful for me to see.

I give her a hug and feel how fragile she feels against me – like maybe she could just disappear in my arms, leaving broken hearts behind who would miss her. Does she even know just how important she has made herself to others? This friend, who I now see is dying. This woman who helped me make sense of the world we lived in as traumatized Indigenous women, and who has made me laugh through pain, is disappearing before my eyes – again.

I am at a loss for words and know the struggles I must have had at the time could not be as imminent as hers in that moment, so I hold in all I want to be released from. She hugs me back, spirit broken, and asks me for a cigarette. I tell her I miss her; I tell her I love her, and my heart is certain she has already died in spirit – nothing left to live for. I imagine I give her the rest of what's left of my cigarettes, get back into my car, and drive away, sensing that I will never see her again. I can't stop the sadness and tears, and I cry. That part I do remember, tears turning streets into fishbowls of images, I need to pull over. As much as I needed her then, how could she be available to me, and I to her, if she had already given up? The trauma bond we share, broken.

In our early twenties, over twenty years ago, we would stroll up Commercial walking past mom-and-pop shops, window shopping, pushing our children in strollers, budgeting for lunch at one of the somewhat affordable restaurants and talking about anything and everything two traumatized twenty-three-year-olds talk about. I imagine the topic of sex comes up, but between her and I, what do we actually know about it except objectification? Sexual abuse in care a commonality between two abandoned children trying to fill the role of two functioning adults trying to lead normal lives between bouts of self-doubt, self-hatred, and political racism. I have longed to have those heart-to-heart conversations we had over the landlines, curly cords twisting round and round my finger, releasing and retwisting like meditation and I imagine she does the same as we talk about children, relationships, and laugh about past traumas – like laughing about them made them less threatening and maybe the more we shared with each other, the less it hurt.

I imagine that night, she must have welcomed the darkness – an imaginary buckskin covering that kept her somewhat safe from examining herself in the harsh light of day; everyone rushing off to seemingly important jobs, children, and loving relationships as she hid behind filmy curtains someone else left behind, feeling, just as she was – no one would give her a chance or love her because she was too broken. These thoughts and feelings following anyone around who has suffered trauma, both Ancestral trauma that flows through the veins of its successors, and new traumas brought about by systems indoctrinated in political racism. J and I had both.

2020

This day arrives, where we can sit and break bread together as she agrees to an interview with me about how far in the wrong direction we didn't go – a living, breathing miracle and we both know we dodged many bullets. I have known J for almost thirty years, watching each other struggle through parenting, self-esteem, relationship problems, guilt, loneliness, and resilience. We are still here, living, breathing testaments to the power of Ancestral prayers, hopes, and the power of children and their ability to make you want to live and create new narratives.

J and her son PD, who is twenty, sit across from me on a sunny afternoon in a grassroots restaurant on Commercial Drive, a wonderful place known for their community events, good food, and pedestrian beer. We all order breakfast with mounds of homemade hash browns, a staple, past and present, in our lives – both good and bad. Gone is the face of a loved one dying and in its place a picture of health, an Indigenous woman who transcended looming death and who basically walked on water for her child, her journey long and up mountain ranges of self-hatred, regret, doubt, loneliness, shame, and addiction. I'm happy to be in the presence of J and PD who remind me, ᑭᓯᒪᓂᑐ kisêmanitow exists or neither of us would be here. There's something about our interconnected relationship and the passing nature of our paths crossing that time cannot erase as we talk about our lives and how much they've changed for the better and how far we still have to go on our healing journeys, me with my writing and J with Culture and Ceremony.

Powwow Moccasins

Gone is P the little boy with the braids who called me Auntie in the sweet melody of a child about thirteen years ago, and in his place is a grown man, with long hair and a gentle baritone voice. I ask J how she first got PD into dancing; she leans forward between bites of homemade hash browns and lets me in on a little secret. "Actually, I didn't, he did," she pauses, looks lovingly at PD, and continues, "When he was three years old we went to a Powwow over in Squamish and at that time I knew nothing … he said, Mommy, Mommy I wanna dance, I wanna dance!" She explains to me the little knowledge she carried about what a Powwow was: "I didn't know protocol so I says to him, I think you have to get moccasins first, and as soon as you get your moccasins you can dance." I imagine this young man sitting before me as a three-year-old, excited at a Powwow, watching all the dancers in full regalia, all the primary colours mixed a hundred times over.

I see in my mind's eye the day she paints for me, sunny, warm, and the anxiousness she felt being around Culture which is something she never got to experience as a child raised in care. She continues to tell the memory through sadness, pride, and certainty and tells me three-year-old PD happens upon a vendor selling moccasins, the joy in her face and voice apparent as she continues to reach back into her memory to extract that moment in time. "He says, 'Mommy! Mommy! They have moccasins,' so I bought him moccasins … Then of course as soon as we put them on he says, 'Now, Mommy? Now, Mommy?'"

I can imagine the immense feelings of sadness and joy, something experienced simultaneously rising from somewhere inside as the welcoming heartbeats of the drum paralyze her in the anxiety of the unknown – there she stood in the middle of what seemed like a thousand people with an excited three-year-old who searches for and finds moccasins. The ones she told her toddler son he needed to dance. I imagine the only thing left for her to do is buy them and let him dance, because keeping promises to children is also a part of healing and changing generations. J continues, "Then they called for intertribal, we went out into the arbour and he danced, and I knew right then and there that this was something his spirit wanted to do." J and I talk about the first time we both heard the drum and the conflicting feelings of sadness and joy and how indescribable it feels to hear mother's heartbeat and see all the proud brown faces dancing for the people, creating a vacuum of Culture and pride amidst the backdrop of the city – a feeling of coming home even though you've never been there before.

Children Are Gifts from Creator

J sits across from me wearing a black faux-fur jacket that matches her need to be unique and yet still belong, something she wishes she would have had as a child. She sits across from me, hair tied back in a thick pony tail, only a few grey hairs mingled in a sea of lustrous black; she stares at me with eyes that have seen so much suffering and so much beauty and says, "I believe that Creator gifted me with PD and he chose me to be his parent because Culture has always played a big part of our lives." Her words remind me of many Elders' words who have said that children are gifts from the Creator and that we choose our parents. I remember being angry at the time, ready to denounce his claims; after all, who would choose an absent alcoholic parent and an emotionally and physically unavailable one who dropped me off with his mom one day and didn't come back? It wasn't until I had my own children that I understood this sentiment. How could such perfect little spirits choose such a dysfunctional parent in survival mode who was always in her past and depressed or always in the future and too anxious, never really being able to be in this moment – this moment right here that could make or break a child? Why would they choose us? Because they are gifts and know what we need, even if we don't know it ourselves. And as we sit here revelling in the possible truth of our children choosing us, it hits home – they are the only reason we can sit here today, across from each other just like we did almost thirty years ago.

Forgiveness Not a Fairy Tale

I have not broken bread with J or PD in about ten years, our lives veering apart as mental health and addiction take us down different paths. We discuss forgiveness and how we need to do it for ourselves too and not just the ones who have done us harm. We discuss how as children, little children, we were abandoned by those we were gifted to. How could we believe we were gifts if our own parents weren't there to protect us or teach us? We talk about the things missing in our lives and how we continually search and searched for things without ever knowing what we were searching for. How can we know something is missing if we have never experienced it, and yet we were always striving for a better something, never really knowing what we were supposed to be striving for? All we knew was that there was a huge void that in a moment could make things disappear forever –

J tells me through tears, "When I was a kid I had no idea what forgiveness was, I had to learn ... I saw a lot of violence, and I knew how to hold a grudge. It was all about, all about survival, so I didn't get to learn things like forgiveness ... through our ways, like Ceremony and Sundance and giving myself to this way of life is lots of sacrifices but lots of good sacrifices and it continues to help our family ... We still have a lot of challenges but the thing is, today my son is able to use his voice, to share his feelings on how things have impacted him, and we still cry." I recall her as a super busy mom, rushing from A to B to C and D, just trying to provide for her son and give him the things he needed when she was still so new to healing, we both were, and how she could beat herself up emotionally with the past? We both could.

J was raised in foster care, a part of the Sixties Scoop that took her from her mother, who struggled with the very same issues many intergenerational survivors suffer through: low self-esteem, lack of traditional parenting skills, cultural genocide, loss of language, loss of immediate loved ones through alcohol- and drug-related deaths, suicides, and sometimes just broken hearts. She talks about how alone she felt and how the search for some sense of belonging led her down many paths, including addictions.

I have met J's mom in the past, a lady who has been beaten with the club of colonialism, who seemed to be scared of her own shadow until you backed her into a corner – then she would come out swinging. Just like my mom, and many moms out there, both dead and alive and still struggling. The real grateful dead, finally at peace – no longer being chased by ghosts they couldn't see, remnants of a North America torn apart by greed, racism, and the concept of ownership.

Ever prayed for death to embrace you in its final arms just so the pain would stop? Ever feel so broken that you didn't even feel good enough to be close to your child? Many Indigenous mothers have felt like this and still continue to feel like this, never understanding why, which is why role models, so humbled, stand and speak in their truth. J does just this, "When I do groups and I talk about our blood memory, I talk about our connection to the grandmas and grandpas, our Ancestors and the earth and why we feel like that, we feel like that because our Ancestors prayed for us just like we pray for our future generations and everything. We remember what it was like to be away from our families, to be disconnected, and we always wanted to be connected and you know and so we understand that and I think that's part of why we feel like we finally belong and I always say that it's a good day to be Indian!" J's beautiful laugh travels the space, she wipes tears from her eyes that have formed from laughter and not just sadness. "It's a good day to be Indian," she says once more with seriousness. "I just feel so proud to be involved in Culture … so Culture and being up on that mountain you have those teachers like Darcy, Calvin, Robert, I learned how to sit with myself, to bear myself, to forgive myself, and it's a process. I was able to sit in that reflection and ask the Ancestors and the grammas and grandpas to help my family, to help us in that gentle loving way to go forward and that's a part of the process."

Her son, now twenty, sitting across from me stealing glances at a woman he called Auntie since he was little – noting all the changes ten years can bring: grey hairs, more-of-me-to-love weight, a few dozen crow's feet, and the same loving, goofy smile he could extract out of me. Many years prior, J and I could not even see beyond a tomorrow and were just trying to survive the day, trying to find ways to will each other to live – after all, if our own parents seemed to not want us, we would find a way to feel wanted. Many years later, we sit together again as we once did, no time seems to have passed, and we have both reached the other side of forgiveness. At one time, we were so angry, forgiveness wasn't even a concept we both knew, and now it's one of the things we are both striving for.

The act of forgiving, not just empty words thrown at our feet to appease the angry child in us, is no longer something we both pretend to practise for the sake of being a normal forgiving person because somewhere down our different roads, we heard that forgiveness will set us free. Now? A very real concept and possibility that we can even forgive ourselves with practice and genuine help from others. We can forgive our parents who didn't know how to parent. We can forgive those that have harmed us. We can forgive our children who aren't ready to forgive us and who still carry past hurts, but the difference from our own lives is that we can sit with our children and just listen, when they are ready. But most important of all, we can forgive ourselves.

Laughter the Only Medicine

One of the things that has gotten J through all the adversity has been laughter, even through the hardships. I offer PD my two bacon which I haven't had a chance to touch, I am too busy giving space to the woman before me, who cries tears of pain and tears of joy in a one-hour interview. In between tears of pain, she recalls a time when she decided to take PD to the Gathering of Nations Powwow in Albuquerque, New Mexico. Since I've known J, I've known that once she decides something, hell has to freeze over before she changes her mind. She walks me through her memory of a scorching summer when she borrowed an old car to take her mom and son to Albuquerque; J turns to her son and asks him to tell me how they got there. PD puts down his fork and says, "We went in a really old car, it was a Chevy Oldsmobile, an '89 or something, and the fastest it would go would be a hundred kilometres downhill and it would only go up to about eighty or ninety going uphill." We all laugh in the quiet restaurant; the waitress looks our way and smiles. J asks PD about the windows and continues through laughter, happy tears rolling down her face. "The back windows were old school so there was no roll-down windows!" She places her hands to show me that the windows opened like flaps. I have missed her stories that can only be laughed at years later. She continues to tell me they had decided to cancel because of a car accident where she hurt her back and PD had a black eye, but her son's insistence to go, she could not deny. I imagine them driving down a long stretch of highway, hot, sweaty, and still in pain from the accident. I can almost see PD trying to stick his little head in the crack of the triangular window flap, to get at least a hint of lukewarm highway air and not the hot air that must have risen around them, making all the passengers grumpy and wondering whose great idea this was. I can imagine all the warm coffees and warm pops sitting in all the old-school cupholders.

J wipes the happy tears building in the corner of her eyes. "We got to the border, border guard asks us where we're going, I say we're going to Gathering of Nations, he says, 'In this car?' (laughs) I was like, 'yep.'" We all laugh at the antics of a desperate mother – desperate to have her son feel proud and to feel that sense of belonging she didn't get to experience until adulthood.

> I remember his emotions (looks at PD). He was the one most excited, because I wanted him to experience what it felt like to be at such a huge event with all Natives and how it feels to be out there because that was his first time and I wanted him to remember what it felt like to be in a huge event like that for our people and to carry that to let that inspire him, to encourage him in that good way and you know that there are Indian people doing lots of great things in their life and that they're sober and walking in that good way, not everybody is out there but I just hope that continues for him.

The memories that J has created for PD will be with him all his life, and I'm not sure he knows at twenty years old just how important it is to have those memories, both good and bad, that tell of a time his mother climbed a mountain with her hands tied behind her back. But one day when she no longer "rocks her mocs," PD will share with someone very important to him of the time they borrowed a car that topped out at eighty uphill and a hundred downhill, that could have broken down in the middle of the US, how his little face with a black eye pressed against the hot glass, and how his mother still made sure he was fed, even if all she could afford was a piece of bannock. I'd like to think he will tell this story this way through the good medicine of laughter.

The Dress

Our hash browns are now cold, congealing, as J tells me about her dress. PD plays a game on his phone, gently reminding his mother of days, times, and different Powwows they've attended where J bought her first dress. There's some light banter around whether it was in Saskatchewan or Alberta that she bought her first dress for Powwow dancing. The waitress refills PD's coke. The sun shines in and makes bright rectangular paths on the dark wood floor. It is a good day to be Indian, sitting across from J and her son PD. I want to hear the story about how she got her first dancing dress because imagining her out in the arbour, dancing for the first time, strikes me as a pivotal change in her journey to becoming the woman I see before me now. She takes a sip of her ice water and asks her son how much it was; PD answers that it was fifty bucks. It seems like a really important point to include in her story and so I ask her to tell me about it. She tells me that she wasn't even planning to buy anything for herself and that they were shopping for PD, always making his outfit more elaborate, and I imagine a time when money arrives from an unknown source like prize money for first or second place at the Powwow in the hot summer months.

J tells me that she wasn't looking for anything for herself and with thoughts of being able to afford PD's dance journey, J wasn't even thinking about herself until, "He said, 'Mom, you should look through the dresses,' and the stuff was bigger, small, or really fancy, and I was just like a beginner and I saw this dress and it was flowered, it kind of called to me, like it wanted me to take it … It was the perfect size, the perfect length, it needed some fixing up … Then PD's like, 'yeah, just buy it Mom, you need a dress,' 'cause he's always encouraging like that, you know … So I bought it. And then I think I danced with it … That's how I started … dancing." She describes the apprehension around spending fifty dollars on herself, whether or not she could afford it, and she also describes the joy. It wasn't a perfect dress, but it called out to her and it needed repairs. The old saying applies, someone else's junk is another person's treasure, and she treasured it. "When I found that dress, I thought it was beautiful but it needed work done to it, I had to redo the back … I had to sew up the missing beads but it didn't matter to me, it didn't matter because I had my very own dress (looks to PD lovingly). He encouraged me to dance, you know I didn't want to spend that money on myself, I wanted to spend it on him." This speaks to her commitment to her child, even through her healing journey, I've known J to put everything, even herself, after her son – those threads of love woven deeply between the bond she knew she wanted to embed in stone so no one could take it away.

She picks up her fork, after laying it down through tears to talk to me about the joys and the sorrows of her journey. She doesn't know exactly where she is going, but she does know how to get there, as she says in a voice clear in reverie,

> It's still hanging in my closet, it's retired now … That's all I could afford at that time and I didn't care. I danced with it everywhere on the Powwow

trail and all the other girls had beautiful dresses that they changed almost every session and every day my dress was still the same but honestly, I didn't care, I was out there dancing and the joy I felt in my heart was … so happy … I always wanted to belong somewhere (says this through tears) … I grew up in care, I didn't grow up with my family, I didn't have that sense of belonging with my family, but there all nations of people could be with my son. I got emotional … I knew that it was a good direction and I knew that direction would help our family … He would have a chance at life with Culture as opposed to what I had, I didn't have any of that, so it was like healing and grieving at the same time.

The End But Really the Beginning

J has this beautiful laugh and her eyes light up when she does it. She has this way with people that draws them to her through her beautiful spirit that she almost lost when she took to the streets, running from the blood memories that seem to haunt anyone who has been kicked so hard in the past that future children fell. She was once one of those future children someone prayed for even before she was born. We were all future children before we were born, destined to be a product of our forced environment – fully acculturated or six feet under in an unmarked grave but by the grace of the universe to have balance, does she stand tall, dance, and pray for the people. I imagine she lets the drums' heartbeat flow through the ground and meets it with every step on green grass, connecting with Mother Earth, spirit, Creator, and the people.

The darkest days in her life, when she didn't feel like living, were when her children were gone, like the mothers whose kids were forcibly removed from their communities to attend residential schools across Canada. J's children are and have always been her reason for living and breathing and continuing to get up every day so they wouldn't have to feel what it felt like to be in foster care with a mother who was on the planet but nowhere near her.

A lot of children grew up this way, no one ever telling them that this wasn't their fault and this was definitely not their mothers' fault either – but the fault of a system designed to "take the Indian out of the child," which meant taking them from their Indigenous parents.

What happens when you remove the laughter out of communities and remove the children who were historically left in the care of Elders to learn oral history and to help the Elders? A symbiotic relationship broken by time, biased history teaching classism, racism, and "self-hatism."

As our visit comes to a close, the sun high in the sky, I see her lovingly look up to her son, who once looked up to her – I think I see PD at three years old looking up at her saying, "Mommy, I wanna dance" – and I think I feel the sadness, like someone in the Ancestral cultural world forgot to send her an invitation. Perhaps when she heard those drums come alive with purpose, presence, and men and women and children singing and dancing like no one was watching, she wanted to be that free.

Her path and mine have crossed many times over almost thirty years, and our stories are similar, yet we have found different ways to heal, me through my writing and her through the spirit of Culture. We have had many conversations in person and on the phone about the Native narrative and how we were so predictable in where our lives should have gone but by the grace of the Creator, do we sit across from each other talking, laughing, and breaking bread; talking about how far we have come and how many years we still have to go.

ᐸᑯᓭᔨᒧᐤ pakosêyimow Wishes

Porcupine quills my children helped their uncle harvest in the summer of 2021
(the porcupine was hit by a car)

Photo by Wanda John-Kehewin

Recovering Catholic i

I eat the body of jesus christ/
wash it down with a plastic goblet of wine –

Suck it down with an elastic gob full of wine/
the sour taste of colonial penance –

The colonial waste and taste of violence/
sits superior in the bottom of my belly –

Shits superiority on the top of my head/
the nun in the habit slaps my hands –

The nun with the bad habit of abuse/
slaps tea-brown children with godly force –

Slapping tea-brown gods with all fours/
taught to her by bible and priest –

Brought to you by libel and beast/
who taught you how to drink cheap wine like priests –

Cheap priests whine and order jc made exactly like bannock/
i eat the body of jesus christ –

Sweetgrass

smell of lit sweetgrass
burned to memory
every day but Sunday
ᗞᐦᑯᑦ nohkom's braid burning
as she circles east to west
murmuring a mantra
praying for her children
and lost grandchildren
praying for peace
and praying they come home
alive –

ᗞᐦᑯᑦ nohkom ᗷᐯᓴᒍ kâkîsimo
to have pity on us, to carry us –

they took her two-year-old boy
to the hospital and brought him back when
he was five starving for
food and affection.
they shackled him to his crib
for three years
and when he came home
he couldn't speak.

my cousin once drove for a year with no insurance
the indian messiah Sweetgrass hung from the mirror, ᐊᔅᒥᐦᐊᐃᐧᐣ ayamihâwin

an invisible sweet-smelling ᑭᓴᒪᓂᑐ kisêmanitow cloak of surety, poverty, and luck.
following ᑭᓴᒪᓂᑐ kisêmanitow's law until we can afford otherwise.

nokum's soft store-bought mocs
scraped, always scraped
the peeling linoleum floor
and no matter how much
she washed it. it was still broken.
deerskin on peeling linoleum
and not Mother Earth;
her whole world altered.
her breathing laboured
her life laboured
from walking
breathing
and ᏥᏈ kâkîsimo
begging for mercy
for all the lost children
roaming the cities, bars
and pool halls,
journeying the jails,
writing their initials on walls
I'M STILL HERE
searching for themselves,
in places where mirrors
tell you if you will succeed
or not –

sweetgrass braid in
three segments
mind, body, spirit
it burns and smoke rises
to the clouds and all the stars
that shine in night sky, were and are
the prayers that gather like troops of ᐸᐣᐹᐧ ᒧᐣᑐᐣ paskwâw mostos

Our ᐊᔭᒥᐦᐋᐃᐧᐣ ayamihâwin can't be stopped.

White Magic

It only took
fifty-one long years
of self-hatred
to start to die out
like compression
of a leaking soul
hissing

Poof!
like a ᐸᐣᵇᐧᵒ ᒍᐣᐅᐣ paskwâw mostos pulled
out of a hat
big, strong, beautiful
brown, wild, and free

Poof!
lots of kids left
after residential school
lots of parents left
before the kids came home,
never seen again like
the disappearing indian act
the last act an indian ever performs
Poof!

Poof!
ᐸᐣᵇᐧᵒ ᒍᐣᐅᐣ paskwâw mostos killed off to ensure instant
obedience or surely slow death
rosary in hand by desperate choice
if our creator can't save us –

maybe theirs can
look at all they possess
pretty beads and flour and thing!
mine! mine! mine!

Poof!
like magic bannock
we rise –

Recovering Catholic ii

jesus christ tasted just like bannock/
The priest put the body of christ in my mouth –

christ put the body of the priest in my mom's path/
his robe whiter than ᑊᐅᐦᑯᒋᒃ nohkom's bleached sheets –

His skin whiter than ᑊᐅᐦᑯᒋᒃ nohkom's sheets bleached/
the priest gave them candy for duties performed –

The priest gave them duties to perform for candy/
she wore her best white dress for candy –

The same coloured dress she wore to St. Paul/
when she fell off the wagon and came home drunk –

The priest came drunk and pushed her off the wagon/
she picked up her rosary and prayed hard –

He picked her up and hardly prayed/
gave her bannock that tasted like jesus, penance –

fareWel Glasses

She walked into your store
with a prescription for bifocals,
all the rage in the eighties,
or so she made it seem.

So happy to have something new.

Asked me if I thought she was old.
Of course, I didn't think thirty-two was old,
I said as I looked at my uncreased hands.
I could count fist-clench lines on hers,
like the edges of old fried eggs
left in the pan on welfare day
because we had more than enough –

Today.

Do these make me look old?
They frame her face.
I see how she looks at me –
expectantly like I'm her hope
and I am.

I have always said nice things to her
  so she wouldn't leave.

They look great on you.
I readjust them on her ears
a little higher on her nose.
I think I'll get these, my girl.
Those are nice glasses, Mom!
Fight Flight Freeze Fawn Fawn Fawn

My mother, both hands glued to her
beautiful new find of purple-fading-into-clear
probably very brave of her
to try something new,
to put all your hope into it,
to feel proud of her choice,
hands her medical card to the storekeeper,
they were storekeepers in the eighties,
the optical illusion man you burst her bubble
bursts my bubble as I watch her become smaller

The welfare frames are over there –

⊲ᐞᑲ·ᵒ ⌐ᐣᗃᐣ paskwâw mostos Bones and Letters

The box arrived in the mail
Raindrops puckering the box
Packing tape east to west
North to south
Slice of second-hand steak knife
Smooth like greasy zipper

Air buzzing like tinnitus
As the quiet held like god's moment
No beginning   no ending
I finally breathed
i   n   h   a   l   e

e   x   h   a   l   e

i   n   h   a   l   e

No, I will not find something
Colonial society
Would want or understand.
Would I even want it?

Dear (insert my name here),
I am sending something to you.
It was from your dad's Medicine bag.
I think it was meant for you.
I think he would want you to have it.

Love,
AD.

I lift out the freezer bag
And recognize
Bone –

Monkey in my brain asks,
"What kind of bone? Is this human?"
What do I know about my Culture?
To warrant this being a human bone.
Perhaps it's my dad's? Naw!
Why would it be my dad's bone.
I watched him being buried.
It's not his.

Drop bone back in box. A note
Tells me it is the leg bone
Of a ᐸᕀᑲᐧᐤ ᒍᕀᐅᕀ paskwâw mostos.
14,000 years old.
A gift to my dad from someone
Who put him on a pedestal
Because he was sober
And he was.

My medicine bundle
Started with a 14,000
Year-old ᐸᕀᑲᐧᐤ ᒍᕀᐅᕀ paskwâw mostos bone.
Thanks, AD.

I Gotta Keep Them Safe

The sun reaches deep into the innards of our borrowed car
with the slow tire leak, two hands grip the steering wheel
like giving birth hanging onto cold-steel bedrails –
like I could control a careening car or careening kid.
I'd like to think I could with a mother's love and hope,
even if I never was taught how to love or how to hope.
Or even how to drive –

They were all too busy trying to make it till tomorrow,
make it till tomorrow, a mantra for the dying,
proof one could die of sadness –

I gotta keep them safe.

My thoughts race wondering if I'll ever
go home again as "hurt people" hurt
others in a slow game of crabs in a bucket.
Like being right keeps you alive
with a false sense of righteousness
learned in english.
Lateral violence a by-product
now being given away for free.

Reservation roulette. I'm a pro.
I just left when I became too good
at reading paperbacks, poverty, and people.

I gotta keep them safe.

Son and daughter sit in the car with me
safer than I have ever been,
warm wind tossing hair, paper, and plastic,

as they eat fast food from the new chicken place.
But at least I fed them, I tell myself.
Reused chicken grease on their shirts
where they wiped their hands.

I gotta keep them safe.

My mother drank herself to death and disease
and I understand why ... so easy to follow suit.

A quenching cold beer on a scorching Sunday
picking sweet apples in the Okanagan orchards of BC
hotter when you are alone with a couple of querulous kids.

Whisky just after a fight about new kids, old kids
divorce and the new wannabe wife who promises not to drink,
asserts her power over others with passive-aggressive eye snaps
snap, snap, snap like you could hurt me with your turtle-snap eyes.

Sherry mixed with Minute Maid,
a high-class drink for the richer days fewer and farther.
Red wine when your kids are in care,
and the social worker tells you you're a bad mother.
Chinese cooking wine when the money is all gone
Made of pure salt ... keeping you afloat.

I gotta keep them safe.

Father died of colon cancer and guilt,
I don't understand like he didn't understand
how to create a bond with my children.
I didn't even have one with you.
Go on home, Dad.

Dad the three-letter word next to dog and god.

I'll read about attachment in about thirty years, I should have said.
Then I remember you went to day school and how Mr. Brosseau
would hurt the boys and I take it all back.
Thank you for the dollar, Dad.
Thank you for taking me to the store.
Thank you for not forgetting about us altogether.
I'm sorry for what Mr. Brosseau did, Dad.

I gotta keep them safe.

So at fourteen, I leave it all behind with only a few
articles of clothing, black eyeliner, thirty dollars,
and a deep longing to feel something other than self-loathing
and hitchhike away
just like my mom
and many other moms.

I gotta keep me safe.

Dead Porcupines Aren't Just for Jewellery

I call my cousin and tell him we
found a dead porcupine on the road.

My son, twenty-one, picks it up with a blanket
carefully as if this warm body might
just pop back alive and shoot him
full of white-and-black barbed quills.

We learn porcupines do not shoot quills
but gently curl into a ball, quills standing tall
and so whatever lands its bite
gets a face full.

Porcupines must be really afraid
when they curl into a ball knowing
there are sharp teeth getting ready to
take a bite.

Must be hard to trust your
own ability to protect yourself
baby porcupine, baby girl.

We all stare at this porcupine
lying on a table, clouds hanging overhead.
My cousin, who I call brother,
tells us that it is a baby porcupine.
Tells us we won't get many quills or golden hairs.

Not sure why I picked it up.
I don't make jewellery. I don't create art.
I don't Powwow dance.
I write poems.

He tells us we still have to treat this animal with respect
and picks the baby up by its tiny paws.
Tells us, this is how you pick up a porcupine.
He gently lays the baby back down on the table.
Shows us how to pull the quills out one by one,
Be careful not to get pricked by the quills.
If you do, wash it very carefully, clean it with alcohol.

My sister-in-law gently handles the baby porcupine
with respect and takes her time to gently show our children
how to treat an animal and how to process a dead baby porcupine.
They think it's gross, but they listen because they are loved
and also know how to love back.

My brother, so gentle, so kind, with a penchant for days gone by
wants and commands a gentle kind of respect because of his passion
and willingness to learn how to treat the living and the dead.
As Indigenous peoples, walking close to the Earth, walking softly,
my brother teaches the kids to care for the baby porcupine
even in death –

Dig-Knit-Tea on a Turquoise Platter

Hey you there
Hey
You
There

Can you pass?
Me a cup
Of reconciliation?

I would like   2   start working   on   my   des-sert-ta-shun

Hey   you   there

Can you pass
Me my children

I would like   2   start working   on   my   gene-he-all-oh-gee

Hey
You there
Me here
Pass me my dig-knit-tea

On a turquoise platter PLEASE

mother died: swallowed her tongue in a dream

After Lucille Clifton

the ghost was in my bedroom
wearing thin.

she closed her eyes
to let the darkness in.

then he went to the band office
and begged for gas money.

the first thing he fixed
 after she died was her tongue.

all her broken body parts
sent to the morgue.

Isolation with an Eight-Year-Old

Mom!   Mom!   Mom!
Come play with me!
You have to play
With
Me!

You're my mom!

Mom!   Mom!   Mom!
Why do you always
Do homework
What
About
Me?

Mom! Mom! Mom!
The cat scratched me!

Mom? Mom? Mom?
Where's the cat?

Mom!   Mom!   Mom!
I'm hungry! I'm dying!
Really

Hungry!
Mom!
Can I have juice?

Mommommom!
My favourite time of day
Is lying in bed with you.

Mom?
Let's tell jokes!
Knock Knock!

Who's there?   who's there?   who's there?!
Frog!
Frog who?
Don't open the door
You're scared of frogs!
HAHAHAHAHAHAHAHAHAHAHAHAHAHAHAHAHAHAHA!

Gulp ... I think I would open the door to a frog
And even kiss it!

If isolation
Went

Away

ᑭᓴᑭᐦᐃᑎᐣ kisâkihitin

the most important
phrase in ᓀᐦᐃᔭᐁᐧᐃᐣ nêhiyawêwin
ᑭᓴᑭᐦᐃᑎᐣ kisâkihitin
never lost
despite the
genocide
of people
and spirit
ᑭᓴᑭᐦᐃᑎᐣ kisâkihitin
every ᓀᐦᐃᔭᐤ nêhiyaw
person
knows
ᑭᓴᑭᐦᐃᑎᐣ kisâkihitin

ᑭᓴᑭᐦᐃᑎᐣ kisâkihitin
We have
all heard
this once
in our life
time in ᓀᐦᐃᔭᐁᐧᐃᐣ nêhiyawêwin
ᑭᓴᑭᐦᐃᑎᐣ kisâkihitin –

(**ᑭᓴᑭᐦᐃᑎᐣ kisâkihitin** – "I love you" or "you are loved by me")

ᓂᑭᐦᒋ ᐋᓂᐢᑯᑖᐹᐣ nikihci-âniskotâpân
The Talking Dead

My son Kiyano standing outside of Blue Quills residential school,
which he never has to attend

Photo by Wanda John-Kehewin

ᐅᐱᒫᐃᐧᐤ ᑭᐦᐁᐤ okimâwiw kihêw

These hands have held
newborn babies
and dying loved ones –

I watched them starve
I watched them beg to die
I watched them look to me
hopeful eyes dimming like dying fireflies
on the plains where we had to
leave them. Bury them. Say goodbye.

Children's laughter no longer
carrying across the grasslands.
Same vacant eyes in life
as in welcoming death.
The only difference is
that you no longer believe
in me.

My people, my family,
there is no ᐅᐦᐃᐧᔭᐁᐧᐃᐧᐣ nêhiyawêwin word for I'm sorry.
Why would we need to be sorry?
If we just followed Mother Earth
and ᑮᐧᓭᒪᓂᑑ kisêmanitow.
We didn't need to say sorry. We thanked
we thanked   we thanked   we thanked

We even thanked
when they took our land
and gave us flour, sugar, and lard.
Passport to a new life of sadness and disease
As we begged for scraps

to feed our Elders, our women, and children.
Instead of hunting for ᐸᐣᐸᐧᐤ ᒧᐣᐲᐣ paskwâw mostos.

The competition between tribes
became survival of the fattest,
who had more flour, guns, or horses?
Whoever built a church to get land
became not so underfoot anymore
but an example and colonizer's pet
and perhaps given a small dose of empathy
or perhaps it was "I told you so" sympathy
for the poor souls who would listen
Like naughty children turned around by
Conditioning and reconditioning.
Like a good Indian turned.
Like a good Indian turned – forced to receive a new mother.
A new hegemony replaced Ceremony
and for a few laughable bags of flour –
Did turn men against each other.
Brothers and sisters,
I understand
But now, if you do nothing – I won't understand.

Five Dollars a Year

Inspired by Layli Long Soldier's poem "38"

Years spent searching for answers, and this is only one piece of the puzzle:
the language I use is not chief kihêw's native tongue, nor is it mine.
nanihkâcacimowin of nêhiyawak People who roamed Turtle Island.
I will be writing it through a **nêhiyaw** lens with most words taught to me by a nun
and by parents, grandparents, aunts, uncles, brothers, cousins who went to
residential school.
A contemporary **nêhiyaw** lens where words like genocide and suicide
obviously appear.
Chief Kehewin was the Chief for about five hundred people; this is probably
an understatement.
The new way of life was coming, coming too fast to change careers.
Being **nêhiyaw** is a career, always working towards survival.
During the 1800s, **nêhiyaw** people were spread thin across Turtle Island
to build railways, to build trading posts, to build churches, to build division.
The fur-trade era caused different tribes to fight against each other for dollars;
it was survival of the fattest and fastest, no room to roam on **nêhiyaw** time.
No **nêhiyaw** time to enjoy the communal family lifestyle and tell **awâsisak**
stories of Creation, ways to be, the importance of family and community.
Warriors were out fighting a war they wanted no part of. Backed
into a corner, anyone would come out swinging with locked fists without keys.
Inch by inch, mile by mile, the encroachment upon their Land and souls
seemed to draw a hatred out of the men and women who thought differently,
who seemed to think the darker the skin, the less you knew and so could be taken
advantage of like an unloved, unwanted foster child taking up space
in a house someone wanted to fill with their own white-skinned children.
Systems put in place to teach pre-eminent position and a controlling God.
nêhiyawak did not know the punishing god feared by the white men who
knew how to judge cleanliness close to godliness;
and brown skin wasn't clean, wasn't good enough to leave alone.
Brown had to be corralled on reservations across Turtle Island, trained
and conditioned to believe their way of life was savage and wrong.

Had to ask for permission to leave the reservations to go get treaty money.
Standing in line for a fin so an rcmp dressed in a red cotton leotard
could make you sign for the five dollars a year while
another rcmp held a shotgun in case, standing guard like a promise.
Signing was a way to count the number of bodies in a band –
I have not collected my treaty money in forty-two years, two hundred ten
dollars, broker.
Didn't see a reason to travel from BC to Alberta for treaty days to collect it.
No interest on the money, no interest in the money, and no interest to beg for it.
I will not stand in line for it, will not sign for it, Mistahimaskwa never signed,
never wavered,
he never wanted to lose Mother Earth to people who didn't know how to treat her.
Stealing her jewels, drawing her blood, and eating her plentiful food like a pig
sitting at the golden table, tangling her hair and trampling tirelessly on her body.
Colonizers throw their old people aside like they are no good anymore, treated them
like pesky rats who needed to be caged up in old folks' homes, taken care
of by people who would go home at night not caring if these castoffs lived another day.
Their grandchildren never hearing stories of how to be, how to walk softly.

I am the Great-Great-Great-Granddaughter of Chief kihêw
His blood runs through my veins. I feel his fire. I feel his anger. I feel his sadness.
I feel his hopelessness as the different bands signed the treaties, head down
being brown.
Treaties for five dollars a year to buy flour, lard, sugar, salt, and alcohol.
Thoughts of suicide as a way out of pain began to surface
like having an option could ease your sorrow. Five dollars a year
Genosuicide –

ᐅᐱᒪᐄ·ᵒ ᑭᐦᐁᵒ ᓂᓱ okimâwiw kihêw niso

Great-Great-Great-Grandfather
your blood runs through my veins
like waterfall

waterfalls can be dangerous
if you do not watch your footing

Great-Great-Great-Grandfather
your Stories are in my daydreams
in my writing of days gone wrong

days gone wrong can be dangerous
if you do not watch your wording

Great-Great-Great-Grandfather
your Heartbreak and Resilience
i carry like witness

being a witness can be dangerous
if i carry it all by myself

Great-Great-Great-Grandfather
your Love for your People
like Mother Earth to animal

can be dangerous
Mother Earth to animal if you have greed

Great-Great-Great-Grandfather
your hope travels through time
carried by stories of dying Elders

dying Elders can be dangerous
stories of belonging die too

Great-Great-Great-Grandfather
i hope you feel the love
that travels through my existence

Travelling through my existence
can be dangerous without a voice –

Hark to the Crying Dead

When do we count the dead that tell true Native narratives?
Fauna overgrown on graves of the millions of ᐸᐣᑲᐧᐤ ᒍᑐᐣ paskwâw mostos and
ᑐᐦᐃᔭᐊᐧᐠ nêhiyawak:
Mothers, Fathers, Sisters, Brothers, Children   gone –
Metal Beasts lay iron over graves in greedy black-gold glory.
ᑐᐦᐃᔭᐊᐧᐠ nêhiyawak kicked aside by colonizers.
Sacred jigsaw bones tossed aside like old tree roots.
Everything in the path killed just for being there and aware.
When do we stop counting loved ones dead or gone missing?
When and how do we stop the continuous kidnapping
of sad brown faces who have nothing but love
for the broken parents who would die happy
if it meant their children's lives would rise above,
rise above their pasts so violet blue-black dark.
All the Ancestor angels would greet them
And their souls would finally rest –

The Last ᐸᐣᑫ·ᐤ ᒧᐣᐢᐟᐢ paskwâw mostos Standing

what would you do if the last
ᐸᐣᑫ·ᐤ ᒧᐣᐢᐟᐢ paskwâw mostos to keep you alive
to sustain you for another cold winter

died

in front of you
killed by the men in red
hired to wait for you
to make a mistake
and to change and enact
new laws
they made every day
to suit their purposes
of genocide
of displacement
waiting for you to misstep
so you could die for
all their reasons

what would you do if you had
to watch your child die
from starvation, smallpox, measles
passed around in blankets
by people who just hated you
hated you for being brown
hated you for not believing in their ways
while taking their flour, lard, and salt
because your whole community was starving
not believing in their white papers
made from trees they cut down and
spent mere hours making a treaty

out of what they wanted
and by the grace of god and the queen
apparently
spared some and crucified others

what would you do if your children were
forcibly taken from your home
and put in boarding schools to learn new ways
and told they were dirty savages
told they were dirty
told their language was a sin
told that their hair was disgusting
beaten for speaking their mother tongue
what would you do?

what would you do if the rcmp drove
your child to an industrial area
dropped them off in minus-40 weather
with no jacket or shoes
and they died knowing
they couldn't say goodbye
the only consolation falling asleep
in delirium
what would you do?

what would you do if you couldn't cry anymore?
if all you could do was pick up a pen and
fight for your right to <"Λ pahpi and Λᒪꓵᕐᐊᑉ pimâtisiwin
what would you do if your only defence was
a pen?

what would you really do?

Line
Breaks

Can make you
You sad

Line

Breaks and

White   space

Saskatoons
Dripping juices
In hot   Sun

Gather some
Quickly before
Season ends
And
Things

C h   a   n   g   e

My mother

Died

Just
As
Summer
Floundered
And saskatoons

Shrunk
And
You
Died

Alone
Line
        break

sEAGULlS

I wanted to be ᑭᕽᐁᐤ kihêw an Eagle
Sent me back as a seagull
Roaming the air and land
Rooting around for food
Looking for handouts
Shooed away like crows
Long ago I lost my home
Nothing looks the same
Roaming the air and land
Looking for belonging
Finding other seagulls
Dead for just existing
Rooting around for fillers
Flour, baking powder, salt
I don't know how to seagull
Nothing looks the same
Long ago lost the land
Gasping to breathe
As air and policy aids in
The death of seagulls

ᐅᐱᒫᐤ·ᵒ ᑭᐦᐁᵒ ᓂᐣᑐ okimâwiw kihêw nisto

When does the defeat stop?
Dried creeks of firewater tears and blood
of fallen ᑐᐦᐃᔭᐊ·ᐧ nêhiyawak who died lost and alone,
heart squeezed tight by
unsaid goodbyes never again hellos,
not able to hold their children again,
to tell them, "I am proud of you
and I will always love you
even in death."

Mistaken for a weak man
instead of a man who could
see a bleak future where
food and water could not save you
if your last breath was hatred, shame, and gasoline –
without children's laughter
to draw you back from the past,
without aunties laughing from
their sacral chakras like the pain
of spiritual starvation
wasn't real –

When does your heart beat
with pride and love
Again?
After they beat you
with a silver spoon
and took away your right
to take care of Mother Earth
and only let you go free after
you promised to die –
An unfilled promise to Mother Earth

that will haunt us in 2022
and beyond –

When the country has thrown you
in a jail cell built just for you
muted of colour, of children's guttural laughter,
of a woman's love and touch,
your very own place of haunted meditation –
And your people have left you
and your son, your namesake,
has made his mistakes on public record
so they say
and you have suffered like any loving
parent would and swallowed your child's
mistakes like love medicine gone sour –

The tears flow from different eyes,
as they draw your hollowed face,
like jesus's brother unrealized,
and painstakingly drawn, your pursed lips,
the black eyes, obscurer than crow's back,
with unshed weeping,
even at your mother's graveside,
no time to cry if you want
to save the children –

Your face, your eyes
I see in my dreams
and I write about you in
red-tongued daydreams –
a piece of the past,
I want to understand,
have to understand,
and chew like gristly meat –
the truth buried in my searching gut,

nourishment for my spirit:
to understand how
all of this
was not ours to bear
and the shame of
being born brown
as over-ripened saskatoons
was not a sin.

I feel you, Great-Great-Great-Grandfather
With every hair sketched
painstakingly by someone
who is trying to understand,
trying to learn,
his daughter is your granddaughter,
Surreal and real,
You are alive in my daughter –

Chief Mistahimaskwa

Great   Great   Great
Grandfather
heartbeat
on the heaths
still beating
like ᐸᗂᐷ·ᵒ ᒍᐢᗑᐢ paskwâw mostos hooves
on ᑭᔑᒪᓂᗑ kisêmanitow's land.
Your dream of freedom
still a dream for thousands.
We haven't given up.
We still try
Grandfather
to tell the tale
of a time
when ᗟᐟᐃᐷᐊ·ᐧ nêhiyawak
were free –
free from sorrow.
We see you
We hear you
Your death
an obligation
to at least try
behind torrents of tears.
You died.
Alone.
Grandfather
I am still here.
Pen in hand.

Mistahimaskwa's Golden Shovel

"We want none of the Queen's presents: When we set a fox trap we scatter pieces
of meat all around but when the fox gets into the trap we knock him on the head."
    —*Chief Mistahimaskwa*

It's always been him, he, not we
Alone, always leaving him to want
A small slice of the pie, getting none
Leaving him cold and afraid of
What they are asking of him, the
Wards and the children of the queen
Flour and sugar her only presents
His people dying by the murders, when
Will it not only be he and him and maybe we
The lives of the future children, the trap is set
In the hearts and minds of colonizers, a
Tongue so slimy and more slippery than a fox,
Sign the treaties, it's really not a trap
They said as smallpox ravages we
Fall like flies in cold, wingless and scatter
Chasing dreams and puzzle pieces
Of a time when we trusted equality of
Colour. The last of the ᐸᕁᐧᐤ ᒧᐢᑐᐢ paskwâw mostos's meat
Long gone and the memory is all
They have left as they cook around
The fire, bannock, water, lard, salt, sugar
Cause diabetes but
They are starving as their bodies crumble when
The sugars burrow into their organs, the
Toxic amylase flares like flaming fox
And the blood gets
Caramelized and slow moving into
Hopelessness, helplessness the
Deed has been done, signed, a trap

It has always been he, not we
Left in a jail cell to knock
On Creator's door, just him
On a ghostly prayer in
Times when spirits fled the
Heart and landed in the head.

Intergalactic Star

wind
whizzing
wheezing
past my ear
past my year

I am home

back to memory
bad memory dead
counselling logic
beating new horse

word on page
I see you
I forgive you
standstill Sunday
sun cradling sky
newborn in healing
watching waiting
whole like light
squinting in reaction
still in pain
I still see you
intergalactic star
that
fell from sky

shhhhhhhhhhhhhhh

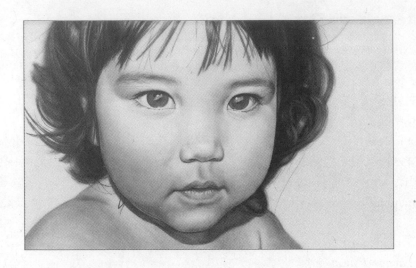

Gary Alteza, *Miya Alteza (2.5 years old)*, 2020

ᑐᐦᐃᔭᐍᐃᐣ NÊHIYAWÊWIN GLOSSARY

I have always felt like there was something missing as I carefully constructed poems in English. I was angry in English, writing about colonialism, and even angrier that I could not express that anger in ᑐᐦᐃᔭᐍᐃᐣ nêhiyawêwin – and so slowly I learned ᑐᐦᐃᔭᐍᐃᐣ nêhiyawêwin words … one day I hope to write a poetry book in nêhiyawêwin even if it is only using the words I need to know. ᑐᐦᐃᔭᐍᐃᐣ nêhiyawêwin short-line poems just like summer days on the reservation picking Sweetgrass as the wind blows sound into ear and I listen for the few words I do know and remember –

With the help of my cousin Daisy John and the online Cree dictionary, I can use some ᑐᐦᐃᔭᐍᐃᐣ nêhiyawêwin words and include syllabics. I will be working with Daisy to be able to pronounce some words. Daisy can read syllabics, which is amazing and something she only learned as an adult attending University nuhelot'įne thaiyots'į nistameyimâkanak Blue Quills. Incidentally, it is the site of the old residential school that closed in 1996.

Daisy reminds me that my language is in my blood memory. I believe her; when I go home, my "rez" accent is prominent and I find a sense of belonging in speaking and joking with a thick ᑐᐦᐃᔭᐍᐃᐣ nêhiyawêwin accent. The heavily accented words that spill from my mouth reminding me that at one time I would have been able to speak ᑐᐦᐃᔭᐍᐃᐣ nêhiyawêwin. Decolonizing myself one word at a time is small, but every drop in the bucket counts. Hiy hiy Daisy for your help and willingness to share and speak with me about the birds and the bees and being heard as a Cree! Thank you Randy Morin for the amazing help with the Cree language, both verbal and written; without people like you in the world, the Cree language and nêhiyawêwin would be lost.

âcimostawinân ᐊᕆᒍᐣᒐᐃᐧᐊᐤ		Tell us a story
âcimostawêw ᐊᕆᒍᐣᒐᐁᐧ·		To tell stories
âcimowin ᐊᕆᒍᐃᐧᐤ		Story
askipwâwa ᐊᐣᕓᐸ·ᣠ		Potatoes (askipwaw, single potato)
awâsis ᐊᐁᐧ·ᕀᐣ		Child

awâsisak ᐊᐚᓯᓴᐠ Children

ayamihâwin ᐊᔭᒥᐦᐋᐏᐣ Prayers

êtikwê ᐁᑎᑫ I guess so, probably

iskwêwak ᐃᐢᑫᐘᐠ Women

kâkîsimo ᑲᑭᓯᒧ Pray fervently to Creator

kihêw ᑭᐦᐁᐤ Eagle

kisâkihitin ᑭᓵᑭᐦᐃᑎᐣ I love you

kisêmanitow ᑭᓭᒪᓂᑐ God, the great positive good force in the universe

mamahtâwisiwin ᒪᒪᐦᑖᐏᓯᐏᐣ The object embodying sacred or spirit power (poetically translated as "spells")

masinahikanâhtik ᒪᓯᓇᐦᐃᑲᓈᐦᑎᐠ Pencil, pen

mâtôw ᒫᑐᐤ She/he cries

miyo kîsikâw ᒥᔪ ᑭᓯᑲᐤ It's a good day

moniyâwak ᒨᓂᔮᐘᐠ White people

mosôm ᒧᓲᒼ Grandfather (nimosum, for my grandfather)

nanihkâcacimowin ᓇᓂᐦᑳᒐᒋᒧᐏᐣ The act of telling a story reluctantly

nêhiyaw ᓀᐦᐃᔭᐤ A Cree man, a native of the Cree Nation

nêhiyawak ᓀᐦᐃᔭᐘᐠ Cree people

nêhiyawêwin ᓀᐦᐃᔭᐌᐏᐣ The Cree language

nikâwês ᓂᑲᐏᐢ Aunt

nikâwiy ᓂᑲᐏᐩ My mother (nimâmâ ᓂᒫᒫ my mom, French influence [Michif])

nikihci-âniskotâpân ᓂᑭᐦᒋ ᐋᓂᐢᑯᑖᐹᐣ The talking dead (poetic translation)

nimâmâ ᓂᒫᒫ My mama

nipâpâ ᓂᐹᐹ My papa

niso ᓃᓱ Two

nisto ᓂᐢᑐ Three

nitôtêm ᓂᑐᑌᒼ Friend

niya ᓂᔭ Me

nohkom ᓄᐦᑰᒼ My grandmother (these days people say "kokom," language is ever-changing)

nohtâwiy ᓄᐦᑕᐏᐩ Father

okimâwiw ᐅᑭᒪᐏᐤ Kehewin (originally it was okimawiw kihêw and was changed to Kehewin due to the colonizers not being able to pronounce kihêw)

pahpi ᐸᐦᐱ Laugh

pakosêyimow ⊲ᑯᔆᐩᒍᵒ	She/he hopes (poetically translated as "wishes")
paskwâw mostos ⊂ᐵᑊᣞᣟᵒ ᒍᐴᑐᐵ	Buffalo
pimâtisiwin ᐱᒖᑎᣞᐱᐧᐁᐧ	Live
sîsîp ᣞᣞᐩ	Duck
wahkômâkan ⊲ᐧᐦᑯᒐᐸᐵ	Cousin
wâpos ⊲ᐧᐳᐵ	Rabbit
wiyasiwêwina ᐁᣞᣞᐧᐁᐧᐱᐧᐁᐧ	Governmental laws

"There is no Cree word for 'I'm sorry'": namôya ohcitaw, meaning "not on purpose," is the closest.

"Papa is French, therefore nipâpâ and nimâmâ is French and Cree put together, which is also called Michif. When the French colonizers set foot on our lands they took in Cree wives as they left their wives behind where they came from."

—Daisy John

ACKNOWLEDGMENTS

I am thankful to have studied under Kevin Chong, Alison Acheson, Bronwen Tate, Sheryda Warrener, Dina Del Bucchia, Bryan Wade, Sara Graefe, Linda Svendsen, and Taylor Brown-Evans, who taught me a lot about writing.

I also offer my gratitude to Layli Long Soldier, who answered the call! Layli so delightfully let me interview her about her creative processes and her poetry and also inspired two pieces in this collection, "Five Dollars a Year" and "Confusion." Layli's poetry collection *Whereas* inspired me to think outside the colonial box and to create new pieces defying conventional rules of punctuation and rules of stability. I will forever be grateful to her for giving me permission to attach her poetic word-warrior name to the poems inspired by her journey. I thank you from the bottom of my Indigenous Soul.

Special thanks go to my beautiful children, all five, who carry the intergenerational trauma with flair, acceptance, patience, and a sense of humour that carries us all through. Thanks to Grace Woo for all you do for my little family and for hanging on for dear life with us and for providing a wall to hang onto.

Thank you, Victor John, of Kehewin, for always believing in me and for always supporting my educational pursuits. I am humbly grateful.

If I have forgotten anyone, it is not intentional, because there are so many more people who I owe gratitude to. If you have ever made me smile, then this acknowledgment includes you! Thank you to Catriona Strang, fellow poet, master editor, and thought provoker! And lastly to all the beautiful folks at Talonbooks for the continued support of my work.

BIBLIOGRAPHY

Adams, Evan, and Warren Clarmont. "Intergenerational Trauma and Indigenous
Healing." *Visions Journal* 11, no. 4 (2016): 7–9. www.heretohelp.bc.ca/sites
/default/files/visions-indigenous-people-vol11.pdf.

Assembly of First Nations / Assemblée des Premières Nations. *Dismantling the Doctrine
of Discovery*. January 2018. www.afn.ca/wp-content/uploads/2018/02
/18-01-22-Dismantling-the-Doctrine-of-Discovery-EN.pdf.

BBC News. "Dozens More Graves Found at Former Residential School Sites."
February 16, 2022. www.bbc.com/news/world-us-canada-60395242.

The Canadian Encyclopedia. "Timeline: Indigenous Peoples." Accessed December 15,
2021. www.thecanadianencyclopedia.ca/en/timeline/first-nations.

———. "Timeline: Indigenous Suffrage." Accessed January 3, 2022.
www.thecanadianencyclopedia.ca/en/timeline/indigenous-suffrage.

———. "Timeline: Residential Schools." Accessed December 22, 2021.
www.thecanadianencyclopedia.ca/en/timeline/residential-schools.

Canadian Geographic. "History of Residential Schools." Indigenous Peoples
Atlas of Canada / Atlas des peuples autochtones du Canada. Accessed
December 12, 2021. indigenouspeoplesatlasofcanada.ca/article/history
-of-residential-schools/.

Facing History & Ourselves. "'Until There Is Not a Single Indian in Canada.'" Last
updated July 28, 2020. Accessed December 12, 2021. www.facinghistory.org
/en-ca/resource-library/until-there-not-single-indian-canada.

Hall, Anthony J. "Royal Proclamation of 1763." *The Canadian Encyclopedia*, February
7, 2006. Last edited August 30, 2019. www.thecanadianencyclopedia.ca/en
/article/royal-proclamation-of-1763.

Hay, Travis, Cindy Blackstock, and Michael Kirlew. "Dr. Peter Bryce (1853–1932):
Whistleblower on Residential Schools." *Canadian Medical Association
Journal* 192, no. 9 (March 2, 2020): E223–E224. doi.org/10.1503/cmaj.190862.

Indigenous Awareness Canada / Sensibilisation aux Autochtones Canada. "What Are Treaty Rights?" Accessed December 12, 2021. indigenousawarenesscanada .com/indigenous-awareness/what-are-treaty-rights/.

Indigenous Foundations. "Bill C-31." First Nations Studies Program, University of British Columbia. Accessed December 16, 2021. indigenousfoundations .arts.ubc.ca/bill_c-31/.

———. "Sixties Scoop." First Nations Studies Program, University of British Columbia. Accessed December 18, 2021. indigenousfoundations.arts.ubc .ca/sixties_scoop/.

———. "The White Paper 1969." First Nations Studies Program, University of British Columbia. Accessed January 3, 2022. indigenousfoundations.arts.ubc.ca /the_white_paper_1969/.

Indigenous Corporate Training. "Indigenous Title and the Doctrine of Discovery." *Working Effectively with Indigenous Peoples*® (blog). January 26, 2020. www .ictinc.ca/blog/indigenous-title-and-the-doctrine-of-discovery.

———. "A Look at First Nations Prohibition of Alcohol." *Working Effectively with Indigenous Peoples*® (blog). October 20, 2016. www.ictinc.ca/blog /first-nations-prohibition-of-alcohol.

Jones, Robert Leslie. "The Old French-Canadian Horse: Its History in Canada and the United States." *Canadian Historical Review* 28, no. 2 (June 1947): 125–155. doi.org/10.3138/chr-028-02-01.

Miyo Wahkohtowin [ᒥᔪ ᐊᐦᑯᐦᑐᐃᐧᐣ] Community Education Authority. *Online Cree Dictionary / nêhiyaw masinahikan ᓀᐦᐃᔭᐤ ᒪᓯᓇᐦᐃᑲᐣ*. Various entries accessed November 2021. www.creedictionary.com/.

Wilt, James. "Tracing the Geography of Canada's Racist Liquor Control Policies." Canadian Dimension, August 10, 2020. canadiandimension.com/articles /view/tracing-the-geography-of-canadas-racist-liquor-control-policies.

Wanda John-Kehewin is a Cree writer who came to Vancouver, BC, from the Prairies on a Greyhound when she was nineteen and pregnant – carrying a bag of chips, thirty dollars, and a bit of hope. Wanda has been writing about the near-decimation of Indigenous cultures, languages, and traditions as a means to process history and trauma that allows her to stand in her truth and to share that truth openly. Wanda has published poetry, children's books, graphic novels, and a middle-grade reader with hopes of reaching others who are trying to make sense of the world around them, especially if they think they come from nowhere and don't belong either. With many years of travelling the healing path (well, mostly stumbling), she brings personal experience of healing to share with others. Wanda is a mother of five children, one dog, two cats, and three tiger barbs, and grandmother to one super-cute granddog.

Photo by Tammy Jayne Quinn